Dear Parents,
with our colouring book “Mo has to go to hospital“ children who are not able to read accompany Mo, a sick teddy, to hospital. There the children learn that you do not have to be afraid in hospital. By colouring they experience what happens to Mo.
KreBeKi is a Bavarian foundation for children suffering from cancer and other handicaps.
KreBeKi depends on volunteer work and donations.
KreBeKi gives away thousands of booklets to children of preschool c… children’s hospitals.
The translation of this book into different languages has been made … volunteer work of pupils and grown-ups.
We wish you and your children a lot of fun with this colouring book

Gaby Eisenhut, chairwoman of the KreBeKi Foundation

Cher parents,
avec notre livre à colorier, « Maurice doit aller à l’hôpital » les enfants qui ne savent pas encore lire accompagnent l’ours Maurice à l’hôpital. Ils apprennent ainsi à pas avoir peur d’aller à l’hôpital. En coloriant, ils apprennent tout ce qui se passe à l’hôpital.
KreBeki, la fondation pour les enfants atteints de cancer et les enfants handicapés,qui vit exclusivement de dons et de bénévolat, offre tous les ans des milliers de ces livres aux écoles maternelles et aux hôpitaux pédiatriques.
Beaucoup d’élèves et d’adultes ont participé à la traduction en differentes langues.
Nous vous souhaitons et surtout à vos enfants beaucoup de plaisir avec ce livre!

Gaby Eisenhut, présidente de la fondation KreBeKi

الولياء الأعزاء ،
مع كتابنا التلوين " موريتس يجب عليه الذهاب الي المستشفى" يرافق الأطفال الذي لا يعرفو القرأة بعد، المريض تيدي موريتس الي المستشفى.
في نفس الوقت سيستخبرن
انه ليس بحاجة للخوف في الهستشفي. عن طريقة التلوين سيتعرف علي كل شياء سيقع
لموريتس في المستشفي.

اسم الاساسية: KreBeki
الأساس لمرضي السرطان و الأطفال في با يرن يقع تمويله من خلال التبرعات. الأساس يهدي كل عام آلاف هذه الكتب الي أطفال الروضة و الي عيادة للأطفال .
وقع ترجمة هذا الكتاب الي عديد الغات من العديد من التلاميذ و الناس المتطوعين .
نتمنا لكم و خاصة أبناؤكم الاستمتاع مع كتاب التلوين.
رايس الاساسية السيدة Gaby Eisenhut

Moritz ist krank

Teddy Moritz hat schreckliche Bauchschmerzen. Seine Freundin Anna will ihm gleich helfen. Deshalb bringt sie ihn sofort in die Teddyklinik.

Mo is ill

Teddy Mo has got terrible tummy ache. His friend Anna wants to help him, therefore she brings him to the teddy hospital.

Maurice est malade

L'ours Maurice a un terrible mal au ventre. Son amie Anna veut l'aider. Pour cela, elle l'emmène tout de suite à l'hôpital.

موريتس مريض

تيدي موريتس هو في ألم شديدا .صديقته أنّا تريد مساعدته فورا .ولذلك ذهبت به لعيادة تيدي.

In der Aufnahme

Die Krankenschwester in der Aufnahme fragt Moritz, wie er heißt und wo es ihm weh tut. Außerdem wird Moritz gemessen und gewogen. Anna ist immer dabei.

In the emergency room

The nurse in the emergency room asks Mo's name and about his pain. Furthermore Mo is measured and weighed. Anna is with him the whole time.

Aux urgences

L'infirmière des urgences demande à Maurice comment il s'appelle et où il a mal. En plus, Maurice est mesuré et pesé. Anna est toujours là.

موريتس في التسجيل

الممرضة في التسجيل تسأل موريتس عن
إسمه وعن الاوجعة التي عنده .
كذالك سيقع قياس طِول ووزن موريتس .
صديقته أنآ معه طول الوقت

Im Wartezimmer

Teddy Moritz ist nicht allein in der Klinik. Im Wartezimmer warten noch viele andere Kuscheltiere auf die Untersuchung. Dort lernt Moritz den Raben Kuno kennen.

In the waiting room

Teddy Mo is not alone in hospital. In the waiting room there are other cuddly toys waiting for their check-up. There he gets to know Kuno, a raven.

Dans la salle d'attente

Maurice n'est pas seul à l'hôpital. D'autres animaux de peluche attendent dans la salle d'attente pour être examinés. Là, Maurice rencontre le corbeau Kuno.

في غرفة الانتظار

تيدي موريتس ليس هو الوحيد في العيادة
في غرفة الانتظار العديد من الحيوانات
المحنطة الاخري في انتظار الفحص ،
هناك تعرف موريتس علي الغراب كونو

Beim Doktor

Dr. Segerer ist sehr nett zu Moritz und untersucht ihn ganz vorsichtig. Mit einem Stethoskop hört er Moritz Bauch und Herz ab. Das tut gar nicht weh.

At the doctor's

Dr Segerer is very nice (to Mo) and examines him carefully. With the stethoscope he listens to the noises in Mo's tummy and to his heartbeat. It does not hurt at all.

Avec le médecin

D. Segerer est très gentil avec Maurice et l'examine très gentiment. Il écoute le ventre et le cœur de Maurice avec un stéthoscope. Cela ne fait pas mal du tout.

عند الدكتور

الدكتور سِيكَرا هو لطيف جدّا مع موريتس
و يفحصه بكل انتباه
بالسماعة سيعرف ما يجرا في بطن موريتس
و يسمع دقات قلبه .ان طريقة هذا الفحص
ليس موجعة

Die Untersuchung

Dr. Segerer untersucht Moritz ganz genau. Er tastet seinen Bauch ab und schaut auch mit einer kleinen Lampe in Moritz Hals. Dabei darf Moritz ihm die Zunge herausstrecken.

The examination

Dr. Segerer examines Mo even further. He palpates his tummy and uses a little flashlight to look into his throat. Mo is even allowed to stick his tongue out.

L’examen

D. Segerer examine complètement Maurice. Il palpe son ventre et regarde la gorge de Maurice avec une petite lampe. Pour une fois, Maurice peut lui tirer la langue.

الفحص

الدكتور سيكرا يفحص موريتس بكل انتباه ،
وقع فحص بطنه و شاف بمصباح صغير
في حلق موريتس .و طلب من موريتس
بإخراج لسانه

Kuno und das Röntgenbild

Der Rabe Kuno hat sich eine Feder gebrochen. Er zeigt Moritz das Röntgenbild von seinem Flügel. Strahlen haben ein Bild gemacht, wie es in Kuno aussieht. Das war gar nicht schlimm.

Kuno and the X-ray

Kuno, the raven, has broken one of his feathers. He shows Mo the X-ray of his wing. X-rays are some kind of photos that show your inside. Kuno says that the procedure was not bad.

Kuno et la radiographie

Kuno le corbeau s'est cassé une plume. Il montre les radio de sa plume à Maurice. Les rayons X montrent l'intérieur de Kuno. Cela ne fait pas du tout mal.

كونو و صورة الأشعة

الغراب كونو قد تكسرت له ريشة .
يضهر لموريتس التصويرة الأشعة من جناحه
و قد جعلت الأشعة الصورة كما يبدو كونو ,

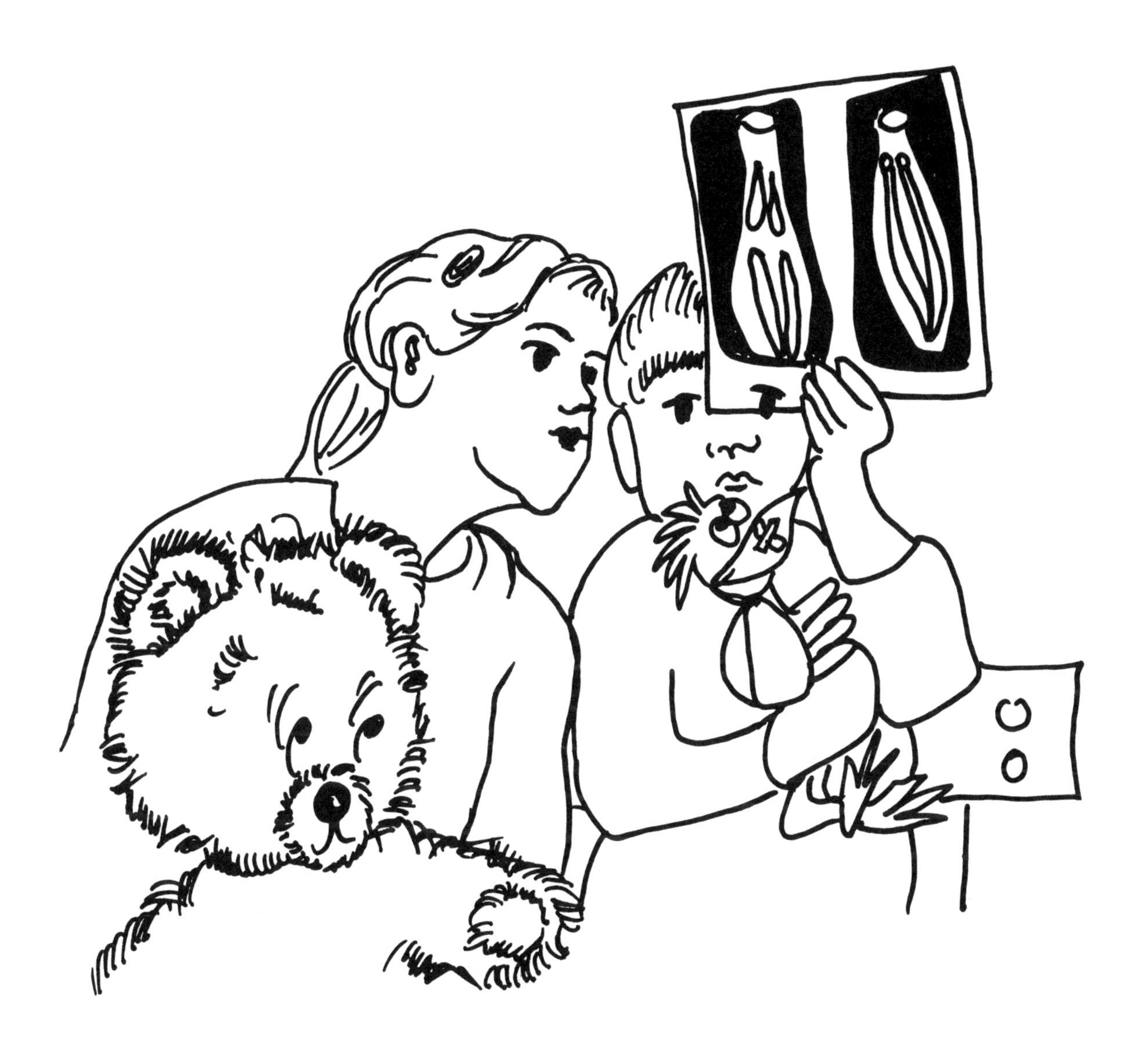

Beim Ultraschall

Dr. Hermann muss in Moritz Bauch schauen. Das macht sie mit Ultraschall. Auf einem Bildschirm kann es Moritz dann selbst sehen: Da ist ja eine Murmel in seinem Bauch!

The Ultrasound

Dr H. has to look into Mo's tummy. Therefore she uses ultrasound. On the monitor Mo can see that there is a marble in the stomach.

Les ultrasons

D. Hermann doit examiner le ventre de Maurice. Il le fait avec les ultrasons. Maurice peut se voir sur l'écran. Il a une bille dans le ventre!

في الموجات فوق الصوتية

يجب علي الدكتورة هارمان للنظر في بطن موريتس .و يكون هذا الفحص بالموجات فوق الصوتية .على الشاشة يمكن لموريتس النضر بنفسه :هناك الرخام في بطنه

Moritz muss operiert werden

Die Ärzte müssen die Murmel aus Moritz herausholen. Sie wollen ihn operieren. Vor der Operation bekommt Moritz eine Narkose. Dann schläft er fest und träumt schön.

Mo has to be operated on

The doctors have to get the marble out of Mo's stomach. They want to operate on him. Before the operation Mo has to be sedated. That means he will fall asleep and have a nice dream.

Maurice doit être opéré

Les médecins doivent retirer la bille du ventre de Maurice. Ils veulent l'opérer. Il est anesthésié avant l'opération. Il dort profondément maintenant et il fait des beaux rêves.

موريتس يلزمه عملية جراحية

الاطباء لديهم الحصول علي الرخام من بطن
موريتس .يحصل موريتس علي مخدر قبل
العملية الجراحية .ثم ينام بسرعة و يحلم
حلما جميلا

Die Operation

Anna darf bei der Operation dabei sein. Sie bekommt grüne Kleidung und einen Mundschutz wie die Ärzte und Schwestern. Moritz merkt gar nicht, dass er aufgeschnitten wird.

The operation

Anna is allowed to be with him. She has to wear a green scrub and a mask like the doctors and the nurses. The whole operation does not hurt at all.

L'opération

Anna peut assister à l'opération. Elle reçoit comme les médecins et les infirmières un vêtement vert et un masque. Maurice ne se rend pas du tout compte qu'il est ouvert.

العملية الجراحية

يمكن لِأُنا الحضور أثنا ء العملية .تحصلت علي ملابس الخضرا ء وقناع الطبي مثل الاطباء والممراضات .موريتس لم يدرك بالجراحة

Nach der Operation

Nach der Operation muss Moritz noch etwas in der Klinik bleiben. Er teilt sein Krankenzimmer mit Elefant Sira. Dem Elefanten wird gerade der Rüssel eingegipst.

After the operation

After the operation Mo has to stay in hospital for a while. He shares a room with Sira, the elephant, whose trunk is being set in plaster.

Après l’opération

Après l’opération, Maurice doit rester à l’hôpital encore quelque jours. Il partage sa chambre avec l’éléphant Sira. La trompe de l’éléphant est en train d’être plâtrée.

بعد العملية الجراحية

بعد العملية يجب علي موريتس البقا ء في
المستشفى .و يشاركه في الغرفة الفيل سير.
ووقع تجبير خرطوم الفيل

Tinka bekommt Medizin

Das Katzenmädchen Tinka liegt auch in Moritz Zimmer. Die Krankenschwester bringt ihr Medizin. Moritz weiß: Medizin darf man nur nehmen, wenn die Eltern oder Ärzte es sagen.

Tinka gets some medication

Tinka, a little cat, is another roommate. The nurse brings her some medication. Mo knows you are only allowed to take medication if parents or doctors agree.

Tinka prend ses médicaments

La chatte Tinka est aussi dans la chambre de Maurice. L’infirmiére lui apporte ses médicaments. Maurice sait que les médicaments doivent être pris quand les parents ou les médecins le disent.

تينا تأخذ الدوا

كذلك القطة تينك هي موجودة في نفس الغرفة مع موريتس .الممرضة تجيب لها الدوا ء .موريتس يعرف :لا يمكنك تناول الدواءإلأ اذا سمحوا بذالك الابا ء أو الاطبا ء .

Bald darf Moritz heim

Moritz wird schnell wieder gesund. Am letzten Tag in der Klinik werden die Fäden gezogen. Damit wurde er nach der Operation zugenäht. Jetzt geht es Moritz wieder gut.

Mo is to go home

Mo gets well quickly. On his last day the stitches which he received after the operation are removed. He is quite well again.

Maurice peut bientôt rentrer à la maison

Maurice guérit rapidement. Les fils sont retirés à l'hôpital le dernier jour. C'est avec eux que Maurice avait été recousu. Maintenant, Maurice va de nouveau bien.

موريتس سيذهب قريبا الي منزله

ستكون صحة موريتس جيدة قريبا .في اخر
يوم في المستشفي سيتم سحب الخيوط ،
هذه اخذها بعد العملية الجراحية
الان ان موريتس في صحة جيدة .

Abschied

Moritz verabschiedet sich von allen Ärzten und Krankenschwestern. Die Kuscheltiere umarmt er natürlich. Er will seine neuen Freunde bald wieder besuchen.

Bye - Bye

Mo says goodbye to the doctors and nurses. The other cuddly toys hug him and soon he wants to visit his new friends.

Au revoir

Maurice dit au revoir à tous les médecins et à toutes les infirmières. Bien sûr, il embrasse les peluches. Il veut visiter bientôt ses nouveaux amis.

الوداع

. موريتس ودع كل الاطبا ء وكل الممرضات
و طبعا عنق الحيوانات المحنطة .انه يريد
زيارة اصدقا ئِه الجدد ،

Das Malbuch „Moritz muss ins Krankenhaus“ wurde von KreBeKi konzipiert und herausgegeben, um Kinder auf einen Krankenhausaufenthalt vorzubereiten und ihnen zu vermitteln, dass sie davor nicht viel Angst haben müssen.

Die Stiftung für krebskranke und behinderte Kinder in Bayern, kurz „KreBeKi“ genannt, engagiert sich auf vielfältige Weise dafür, Kindern und Jugendlichen in Bayern, die von Krebs oder Behinderung betroffen sind, langfristig zu helfen, sie zu fördern und dabei auch durch vielfältige Aktivitäten auf deren Probleme und Anliegen aufmerksam zu machen. Die Stiftungsvorsitzenden und das Kuratorium arbeiten ausschließlich ehrenamtlich und verwirklichen durch Spenden den Stiftungszweck.

Schirmherrin der Stiftung ist I. D. Mariae Gloria Fürstin von Thurn und Taxis.

The colouring book "Mo has to go to hospital" is published by the KreBeKi Foundation for children suffering from cancer and other handicaps. It should prepare children for their stay in hospital and show them that they do not have to be afraid. The foundation provides help for children and adolescents in multiple ways such as long term support and promotion. With many different activities we want to draw people's attention to the problems and concerns of young patients. KreBeKi is based on volunteer work and depends on donations.

Patroness of the foundation is Her Serene Highness, Mariae Gloria Princess of Thurn and Taxis.

Le livre de coloriage „ »Maurice doit aller à l'hôpital » a été conçu et publié par KreBeKi. Ce livre doit préparer les enfants à un séjour à l'hôpital et leur donner confiance à ne pas avoir peur.

KreBeki, la fondation de Bavière pour les enfants atteint de cancer et les enfants handicapés, s'engage à long terme à les aider et les accompagner. En même temps, elle attire l'attention du public à ces problèmes par de multiples activités. Elle fonctionne par bénévolat et la totalité des dons est utilisé pour les enfants.

La fondation est placée sous le patronage de la princesse Mariae Gloria Fürstin von Thurn und Taxis.

لإعداد و تعليم الأطفال حول العلاج KreBeKi تم تصميم كتاب التلوين " موريتس يجب عليه الذهاب الي المستشفى" و تكريمه من قبل المؤاسسة
في المستشفى و لا يجب الخوف منه.

KreBeKi" "الأساس لمرضي السر طان و الأطفال المعاقين في باير باختصار
تساهم في العديد من الطرق المساعدة للأطفال في باير علي المدى الطويل و كذالك لمرافقتهم .
الأساس تريد في نفس الوقت جذب الانتباه
إلي مشاكلهم و مخاوفهممن خلال مجموعة متنوعة من الأنشطة .
تعمل المؤسسة حصريا علي أساس تطوعي و تحقق فوائدها من خلال التبرعات

I.D. Maria Gloria von Thurn und Taxis ظهيرة المأسسة هي

Gefällt Ihnen das Buch?
KreBeKi lebt von Spenden.

Daher freuen wir uns sehr über Spenden auf unser Spendenkonto:

LIGA Bank eG Regensburg
IBAN DE08 7509 0300 0001 3422 66

Mehr Informationen zu KreBeKi: www.krebeki.de

Kennst du schon die ganze Geschichte von Moritz und seinem Krankenhausaufenthalt?

Das Lesebuch ist im Buchhandel oder unter www.care-line-verlag.de erhältlich.

ISBN 978-3-86878-029-1, EUR 4,80

Dieses Projekt konnte mit Spenden der **Maria Ward Realschule der Diözese Eichstätt** verwirklicht werden.

Schon seit 2013 engagieren sich die Eichstätter tatkräftig für die Stiftung KreBeKi. Ein herzliches Dankeschön an alle Schülerinnen, Schüler und Lehrkräfte, vor allem an den Initiator Peter Markoff!

ISBN 978-3-86878-074-1
Best.-Nr. 178048
www.care-line-verlag.de